Collecting the 50s & 60s

Jan Lindenberger

A Handbook & Price Guide

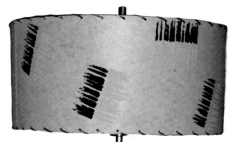

Schiffer Publishing Ltd

77 Lower Valley Road, Atglen, PA 19310

Sun glasses with ear-bobs. 1960s op-art. $115-130.

07233558

Designed by Bonnie Hensley

Title page photo: Ceramic lamp with brass base and fiberglass shade. 24". $50-60.

Opposite page: Angora poodle with ceramic base, rhinestone eyes, and plastic glasses. 9". $35-45.

Copyright © 1993 & 1997 by Jan Lindenberger
Library of Congress Catalog Number: 93-85011.

Printed in Hong Kong
ISBN: 0-7643-0131-4

Published by Schiffer Publishing, Ltd.
77 Lower Valley Road
Atglen, PA 19310
Phone: (610) 593-1777
Fax: (610) 593-2002
Please write for a free catalog.
This book may be purchased from the publisher.
Please include $2.95 for shipping.
Try your bookstore first.

We are interested in hearing from authors
with book ideas on related subjects.

Acknowledgements

I wish to give a special thank you to John and Chris at Firefly Antiques in Manitou Springs, CO, for opening up their shop and home and allowing me to photograph and for giving me much of the valuable information for this book.

Also thanks to the following people and anyone whom I may have forgotten:

Atomic, Denver, Co.

Antique Gallery, Littleton, Co.

Antique Mall of Lakewood, Lakewood, Co.

Antique Market, Denver, Co.

Judy Walton, Longmont, Co.

Rich Vanderhoef, Mountain Man Antiques, Denver, Co.

Myke Johnson, 50/fifty, Denver, Co.

Marlo Rivoli, Denver, Co.

Popular Culture, Denver, Co.

Bill Phister, Denver, Co.

Random Pickin's, Longmont, Co.

Salt Box Antiques, Denver, Co.

State Line Antique Mall, Kansas City, Ks.

Wazee Deco, Denver, Co.

Preface

When one walks through an antique shop and sees the fifties and sixties for the first time, the look is one to be savored. Who would have thought this would be collectible? Those Beatles dolls, the "Brady Bunch Game," Jetsons book, memorabilia from *our* era...collectible? Never! The platform shoes, Fiesta dishes, floral curtains, and even chenille robes.

Unbelievable!

"Who would want that?" you ask yourself. The collectors and the people from the 50s and 60s who used it, of course. No design has been so desired for several years. Furniture was made to use and enjoy. The games and dolls were mostly from T.V. shows, which were a new thing, and most of them had a lot of humor combined with them. Kitchen items had a reason and many new colorful gadgets were on the market. The floors were checkered and the soda fountain look was "in." Lots of red brightened the house, as did chartreuse appliances. The western look for the bedrooms and living rooms were a lively addition as Roy Rogers and Gene Autry were the popular heroes.

All this in the 50s and 60s. Now take a look around today. They have made their comeback. Recently I was at the local department store and saw a lady who was wearing flared bell bottom slacks and a 50s-cut shirt. Now, I consider myself modern. I even have red cabinets and a black and white checkered floor in my kitchen. But flared bell bottom slacks? Never! I do, however, consider them fun collectibles, and everything from the 50s and 60s holds a lot of good memories for me.

When you start collecting go slow and buy what you like and can use. That way you can't go wrong. *Collecting the 50s and 60s: A Handbook and Price Guide* will help you identify your collectibles and will be valuable in pricing your items. The prices reflect the markets in the mid-west and may differ slightly form those in other regions. They also reflect items in the condition shown. As condition and availability vary, so do the prices. Nevertheless, this book will give the collector-decorator a good idea of what an object is worth on the market today. (Please note auction prices may differ from shop prices.)

I hope you use and enjoy this book and wish you all happy collecting.

Jan Lindenberger Colorado Springs, Colorado

Contents

Ceramic bud vase. 13". $10-12.

Introduction

Twentieth century historians will remember the 1950s and '60s as a child of the depression, stumbling from a popular war and its conservative roots, into a mad dash for the future, a cultural revolution, and finally falling into dissent and an unpopular war.

The manufacturers and artists were quick to get in line with the changing times. They played on a new sense of freedom, and an economy based on ever-growing consumerism. Out with the old-fashioned, over-labored designs of previous generations, the over-stuffed floral sofas, the carved whatnots, and the boyish look and line of women's fashion.

The image of the black porter and the mammy became lamp bases of African warriors and Polynesian dancers. Sofas turned sleek and low and textured. The austere "Hollywood Canteen" look was draped with yards of nylon net and fanciful fabrics, revealing the exuberant curves beneath. Steel and wood bent and twisted to the ideals of this new freedom and sense of adventure.

Meanwhile plastic exploded in ever new shapes and uses. The colors that have come to identify the era were new and unusual: chartreuse, pink, turquoise, orange, grey and black, to name but a few. Fiberglass, wrought iron, glass, teak and the lighter woods took on the shapes of the trapezoid and kidney bean and the boomerang. These were abstract and geometric, jet age patterns.

These are the materials and ideals that make the era remarkable and so popular with today's collectors. Some visitors to antique shops with a special fifties department (such as The Firefly Antiques in Manitou, Colorado, which I thoroughly enjoyed) turn away muttering: "My mother couldn't wait to throw that away." Or they just laugh. But everyone remembers the colored aluminum glasses and dealers will tell you they sell like crazy.

Fortunately, an increasing number are beginning to take a second look. Some younger people are seeing the 50s and 60s for the first time, some older people appreciate the nostalgia and can recognize the high design found there. Many are drawn to the simple lines of the bright colors. Others who want the good construction, and still others who enjoy the humor in these artifacts. Not since the mid-Victorian times has a culture produced the variety and quality of the products available from this most exciting and enterprising era.

Figures

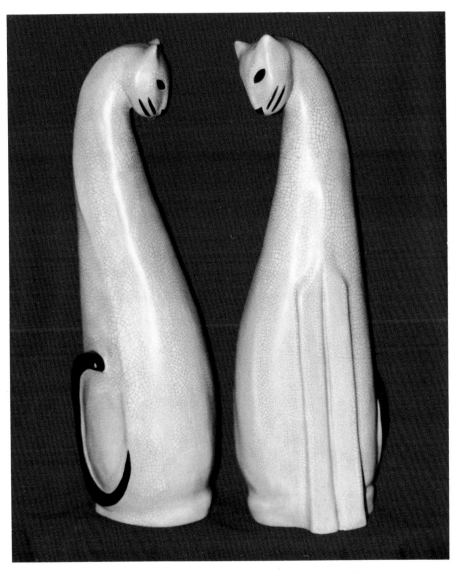

Ceramic cat figurines by Brayton Laguna Pottery Co. 17". $300-350 pair.

Ceramic figurines from Ceramic Arts. Zor and
Zorina. 9". $50-75.

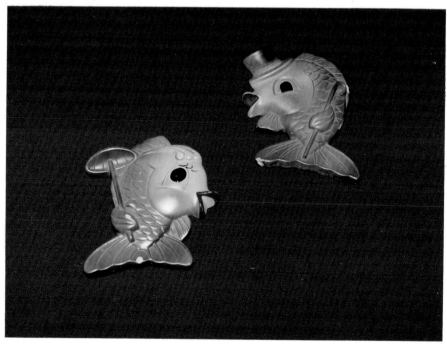

Plaster fish wall-hanging. 6". $12-18.

Pair of Siamese ceramic figurines. 10½". $35-45.

Monkey bank. 8". $40.50.

Beatnik ceramic figurine. 5". $20-30.

Ceramic space man on ship figurine. "Conoco 1958". $25-35.

Toscany clown, Venetian glass, Italy. 10". $100-125.

Lady bug figurines. "Occupied Japan". $40-45.

Plaster oriental girl figurine. $25-35.

"Occupied Japan" Chinese man figurine. 8".
$45-60.

Red clay cat bookends with pen holder, mad in Japan. 7". $20-25.

Ram ceramic tile figurine from Relco, Japan. $25-
40.

Chalk scotty dog figurine. 8" x 10". $60-70.

Ceramic poodle with pups made in Japan. $15-20.

Chalk cocker spaniel dog figurine. 7". $35-45.

Chalk scotty dog figurine. 5" x 6". $45-55.

Chalk German shepherd dog figurine. 6" x 9". $40-50.

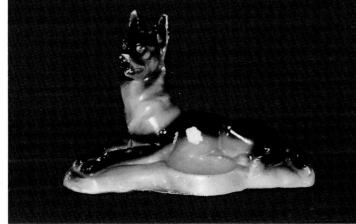

Plaster poodle bank. 12". $15-20.

Ceramic fish planter. 10" x 12". $20-30.

Ceramic swan wall pocket from California Pottery
Co. 8". $15-22.

Gazelle ceramic planter. 9" x 17". $25-35.

Ceramic fish wall pockets. 9". $25-35.

Ceramic goose figurine by California Originals. 8".
$35-45.

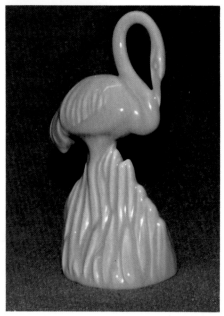

Ceramic flamingo figurine. 7". $25-35.

Ceramic dollar sign bank. 7½". $10-15.

Venetian glass dragon figurine. Italian. $85-125.

Venetian glass rabbit figurine. Italian. $80-100.

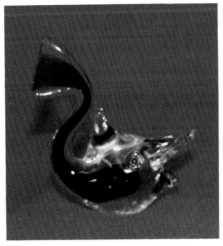

Venetian glass fish figurine. Italian. $80-100.

Beatles dolls. "Nems Ext. Ltd." Rubber, 4½", 1964. $150-200 each.

Rubber toy by Park Smith Corp. Squeeze him and the eyes go around. 6". Synthetic hair. $18-25.

Italian cat figurine. Porcelain. "Rosenthal-Netter Inc." $50-60.

Lucite free-form sculpture, 1960s. $70-90.

Smoking Accessories

Brass, Space Needle lighter. 1962 World fair. $45-60.

"Rosenthal" German lighter made for Ronson Co. $40-55.

Aluminum ash tray with pot metal dog. $18-25.

Ceramic ashtray with pipe in center. "Tilso, Japan". 7" x 9½". $30-40.

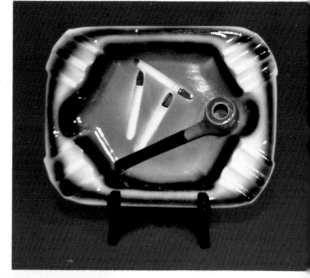

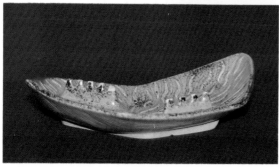

Ceramic California Original ash tray. 7" x 11". $10-15.

Cigarette box and ashtray set. Gold brushed, ceramic. $40-50.

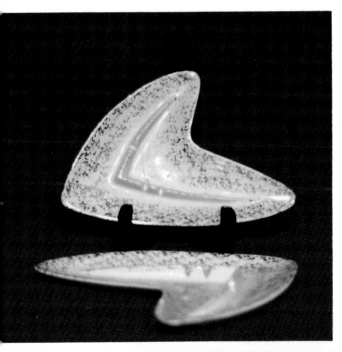

"Shawnee #205" pink and gold
speckled set of ashtrays. $30-
40.

California Originals ceramic
ashtray. #981. 12". $15-20.

Donkey cigarette dispenser. $40-50.

Metal ash tray, donkey holds cigarettes. $20-30.

Bakelite ashtray, U.S.A. $35-45.

Planters, Vases and Bowls

Sea shell ceramic planter. 4" x 8". $15-22.

Plastic planters. $7-12.

Glazed ceramic tiger planter. 9½" x 6½". $20-30.

Ceramic panther planter with jewel eyes. 9" x 14".
$40-60.

Ceramic fish planter made in Japan. 5" x 3". $10-15.

Plastic bowl planter with wire stand. $25-35.

Ceramic oriental figurine planters. $30-40.

"Rookwood" pottery bud vase. 7½". 1961. $60-75.

Art glass hand painted vase. 17". $75-100.

Ceramic vase by Maysel Deter. 4" x 8½". $35-45.

"Rookwood" pottery vase. 4". 1952. $200-250.

Vase by "George Briard". Black with gold etchings. 18½". 1960s. $60-75.

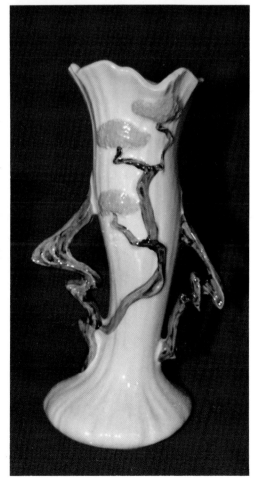

"Roseville" pottery ming tree vase. 13". $175-200.

Ceramic sculptured vase. 10". $25-35.

Venetian glass vase. 12". $120-150.

Drayden pottery vase. $40-50.

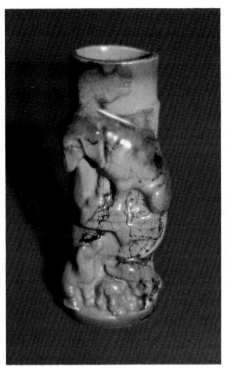

"Ramses" pottery vase, dogs embossed on stump. 7¼". $75-100.

Roseville vase #81.7. 7". $85-120.

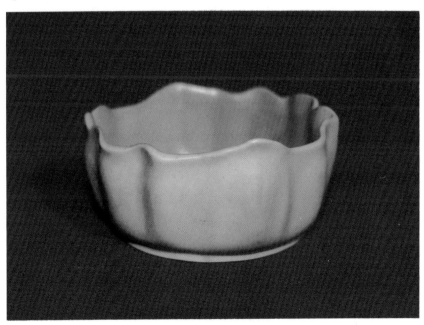

Roseville bowl #60-6. 6½". $70-90.

Decanters

Opalescent blue decanter with stopper. 22". $75-
100.

Jim Beam Colorado centennial decanter. 1959. $60-75.

Hand-blown decanter. 8". Stopper 2¼". $55-75.

Hand-blown and molded decanter in the shape of woman. $150-175.

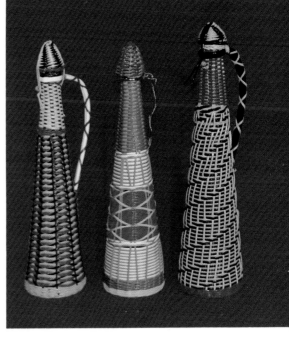

Spanish glass decanters covered in plastic braiding. 15½ to 17". $50-75.

Plastic Crown Royal bottle. 18½". $75-100.

Glass Gordon's gin bottle. 23". $100-125.

Glass Ancient age whiskey bottle. 23". $90-120.

Glass Drambuie bottle. 18". $95-140.

Design with Function

Bakelite jewelry box. $35-50.

Powder box by Lucite, Dupont. $25-35.

Norelco battery and electric travel shaver in case. $45-55.

Set of three cardboard hat boxes. $50-60.

Plastic eye glasses with rhinestones. $30-40.

Brass eye glass holder with rhinestone by Gold Tone
Products.
$20-30.

4 piece plastic vanity set by Mitchell Gould Co. Inc. $30-35.

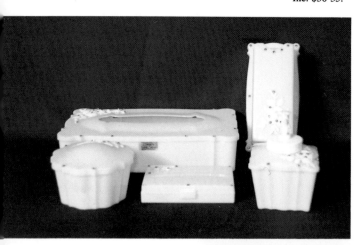

Five-pieced dresser set. $45-55.

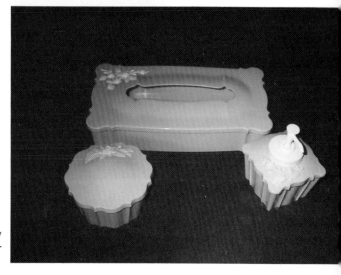

Three-piece dresser set by Schwartz Bros. Plastics. $30-40.

Metal waste paper basket. 13". $15-20.

Quilted child's hamper. 19" x 10¼". $30-40.

Plastic quilted waste paper basket. 13". $20-35.

Wendy, soaky bubble bath by Walt Disney Productions. 10". $30-40.

Snow White bubble bath by Colgate Palmolive Co. 11 oz. $30-40.

Wooden lady clothes brush. 5½". $15-20.

Black boy clothes brush. $60-75.

Black lady clothes brush. $60-80.

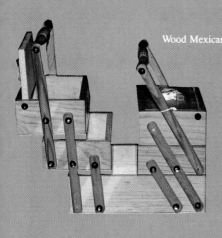

Wood Mexican jewelry box. $40-55.

Frosted plastic powder box by Ciera. $20-30.

Cardboard jewelry box with bakelite. $35-50.

Marbleized plastic box. 5" x 12". $20-30.

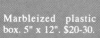

Satin undergarment bag. 15" x 22". $30-40.

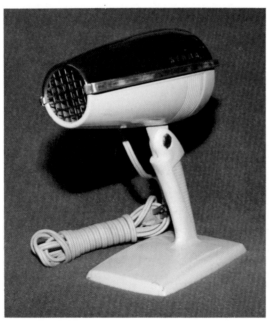

Kenmore hair dryer of plastic and metal. $25-35.

Shaving set by Stanlite U.S.A. $40-50.

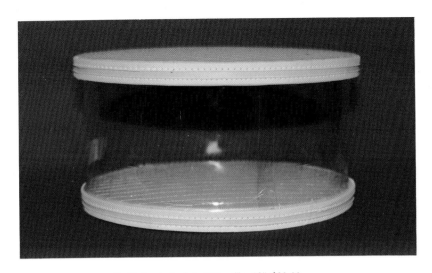

Quilted and plastic hat box. 6" x 12". $20-30.

Glove holders by Handi Form Co. $30-40.

Celluloid speckled soap dish. $15-20.

Clothing

Lady's cotton Nehru jacket. $40-50.

Lady's cotton zebra print dress. $30-40.

Fake leopard jacket. $100-125.

Unisex bell bottom leather suit. 1960s. $50-75.

Quilted cotton lined lounge jacket, with tie. $50-75.

Lady's red satin cowboy shirt. $40-50.

Lady's flannel circle skirt. $50-60.

Lady's cotton, hand-printed Mexican wrap skirt. $60-75.

Cotton print skirt. Size 10. $45-55.

Lady's lavender satin cowboy shirt. $35-45.

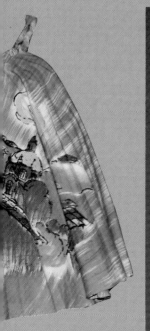

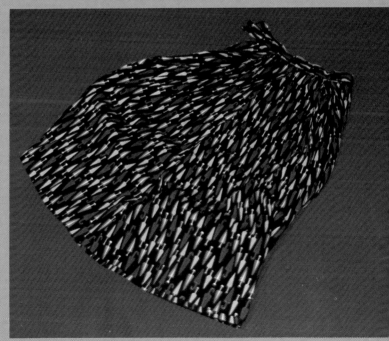

Cotton gathered skirt with umbrella print. $40-50.

Young girl's taffeta and net prom dress. $60-75.

Lame' charcoal silver woman's/man's pant suit.
$60-75.

Rayon two-piece lady's jacket. $50-75.

Lady's leather jacket with attached cape. $60-90.

Lady's dress by Oleg Cassini. $60-70.

Lady's mini wool dress with beads and sequins from Hong Kong.
$50-65.

Man's wool overcoat. Mid-50s. $60-75.

Lady's beaded synthetic fabric coat and dress from
Hong Kong.
$45-55.

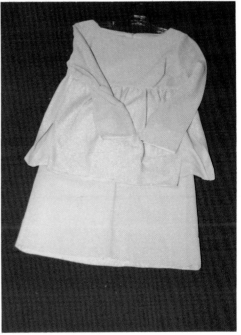

Lady's tulip dress, synthetic lame'. $40-50.

Lady's brocade party dress. $45-55.

Celluloid belt with elephants as buckle. $35-45.

Lady's sequined top with beaded fringe. $75-100.

Paper disposal dress. "Tyrrell Industries, Venice, Fla." $35-45.

Tortoise handle purse with gold lame', folds in half and snaps together. $25-35.

Framed silk tie signed by designer, Salvador Dali. $450-500.

Terry cloth man's beach jacket. $40-45.

Man's cotton Hawaiian style shirt. $35-45.

Woman's shoes with floral fabric from Sedoni, Paris. $30-40.

Woman's shoes. Leopard and vinyl, Condotti, N.Y. $25-35.

Woman's shoes with fabric and glitter by Custom Craft. $25-40.

Jewelry

"Topaz" rhinestone with glass beads, necklace and earrings.
$95-125.

Austrian crystals-glass pendant and earrings. $80-90.

Copper and enamel necklace. $40-50.

Amethyst rhinestone and glass bracelet. $65-80.

Beads and buttons on stretch fabric, bracelets. $30-40.

Rhinestone bracelet. $55-65.

Copper and enamel "Matisse" bracelet and earrings.
$65-75.

Rhinestone pendant and earrings. $55-65.

"Weiss" rhinestone broach. $85-120.

Sterling earrings with owl inlay. $25-30.

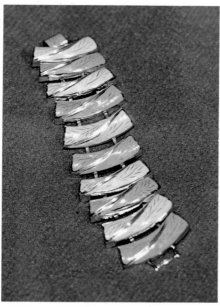

Bracelet, enamel inset into gold ton base. $40-50.

Elvis Presley plated charm bracelet. $200-250.

Charm bracelets. Gold-filled and silver. $40-50.

Lady's sweater guards. Rhinestone and stone inserts. $20-30.

Ballerina pendant/necklace gold tone. "O.R.N.K."
$30-45.

Pendant/necklace base holding several chains. $30-40.

Painted phoenix bird with gold and silver tones, pendant/necklace.
$25-35.

Copper pendant. $15-25.

Bakelite scotty dog pin. $15-25.

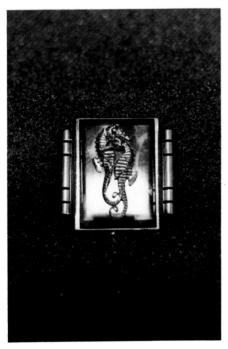

Lady's pin of tortoise shell on brass. "JHP Paris".
$50-75.

Shell pin with Bakelite leaves. $15-20.

Brushed gold tone, marked right and left, cuff links. $7-10.

Imitation marble inlay with gold tone cuff links. $15-20.

Silver tone, "Swank" cuff links. $12-18.

Man's cuff links. "N.F. Silver". $20-25.

Silver tone with amethyst stone, cuff links. $18-22.

Red enamel Siam dancers on silver tone "Swank" cuff links. $25-35.

Cuff links, marked sterling. $35-40.

Gold tone with brushed centers, cuff links. $35-40.

Brushed gold cuff links. $35-40.

Mexican sterling cuff links. "828 Emma". $40-50.

Gold tone with onyx stone, cuff links. $32-38.

Gold plated cuff links, with onyx stone. $50-70.

Tie tack and cuff link set. Aluminum with embossed car. $38-45.

Brass with Roman motif, tack and cuff set. $25-35.

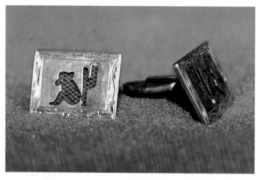

Plated silver, handmade Mexican cuff links. $35-45.

Tie tack, silver tone with dragon on plastic bubble. $20-30.

Brass with pearl insert, tie bar. $12-15.

"Shields" tack and cuff link set. Brushed gold. $30-40.

"Shields" tack and cuff link set. Silver tone with stone inset.
$30-40.

Lady's gold filled glove guard with simulated opal. $25-35.

Plastic charms on a display card. $150-175.

Charms on a display card. "Japan". Metal, Gold tone. $60-75.

The Western Influence

Copper horse, framed. $150-175.

Western ceramic ashtray. Unmarked. 7¼" x 11½".
$45-55.

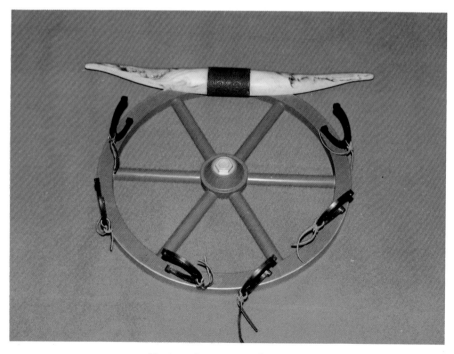

Plastic cowboy coat rack. $75-100.

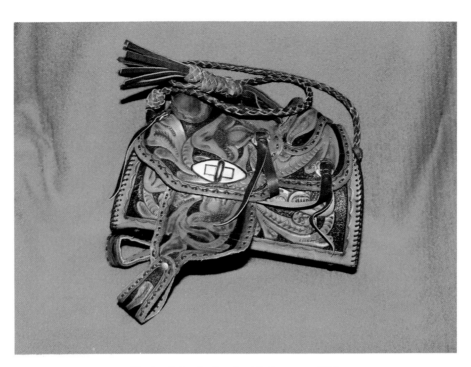

Hand-tooled and colored saddle bag purse. $125-150.

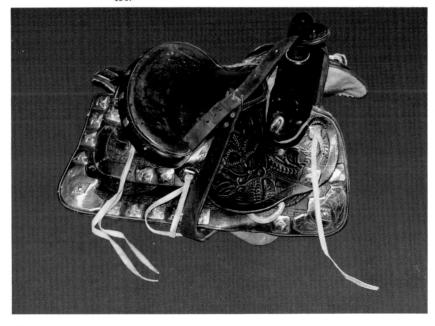

Leather hand-tooled saddle with horse head nickel trim. $275-350.

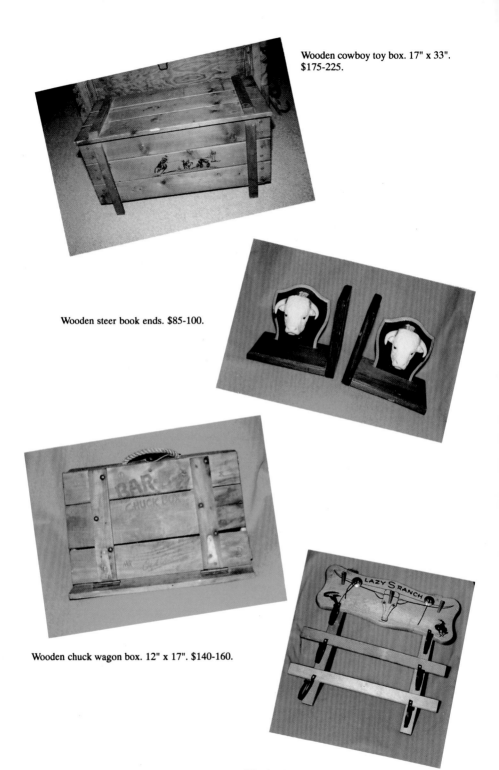

Wooden cowboy toy box. 17" x 33". $175-225.

Wooden steer book ends. $85-100.

Wooden chuck wagon box. 12" x 17". $140-160.

Wood child's coat rack. $75-100.

Colorado state western silk scarf. 28" x 28". $90-125.

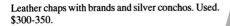

Leather chaps with brands and silver conchos. Used. $300-350.

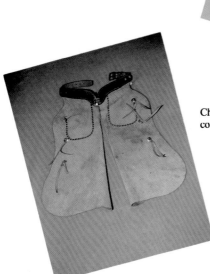

Child's suede and hand-tooled chaps, with silver concho. $160-190.

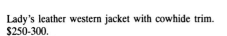

Lady's leather western jacket with cowhide trim. $250-300.

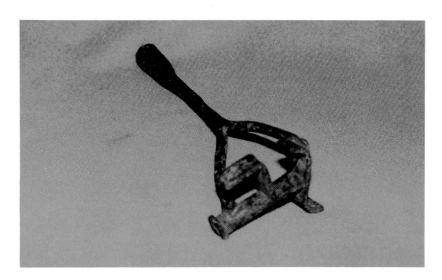

Branding iron "H". 12½". $60-70.

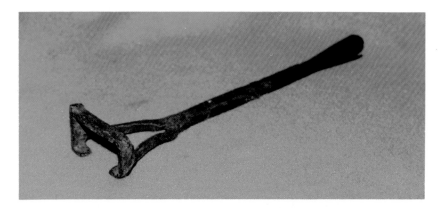

Branding iron "C". 15". $60-70.

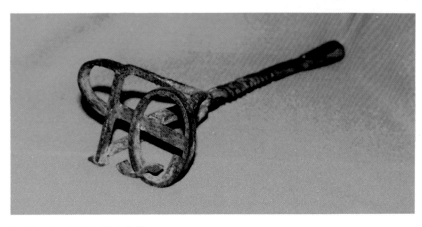

Branding iron "QP". 17". $60-70.

Silver stagecoach tie bar. $25-30.

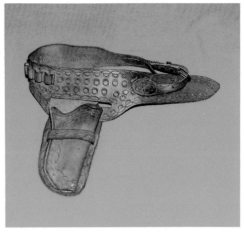

Leather hand-tooled holster. $80-100.

Man's belt buckle. "Comstock silversmiths-German silver". Brass star with silver inlaid horse. $80-100.

Tooled leather rifle holder. 44". $175-225.

Children's leather boots. $55-75.

Blue hand-tooled leather boots. $50-60.

Leather hand-tooled cowboy boots. $60-75.

Lighting

Brass lamp with plastic leaves. 29". $150-175.

Wrought iron stand with frosted glass globe and fiberglass shade. 25". $60-75.

Wrought iron base ceramic lamp with fiberglass shade. 25". $60-75.

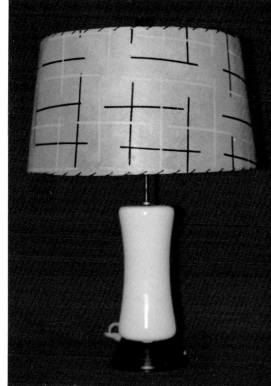

Wrought iron and brass table lamp with paper shade. 23". $40-60.

Wrought iron and brass table lamp with parchment shade. 27½". $95-120.

Three piece wrought iron and brass mantle set. $90-125.

Wrought iron and brass floor lamp with parchment shade. 57".
$250-300.

Wrought iron lamp with light in base and top. 21½".
$100-130.

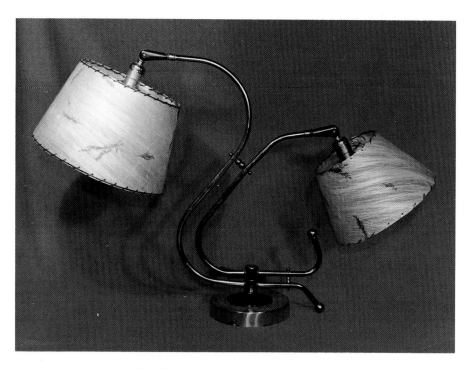

Adjustable double-head brass lamp with parchment
shades. 23" x 32".
$140-180.

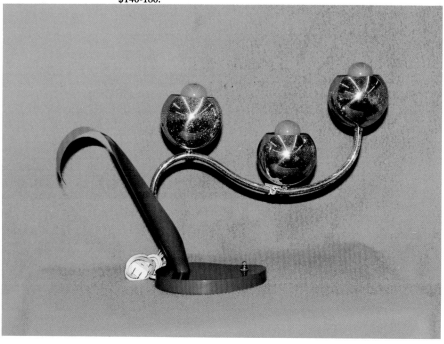

Brass and tin atomic lamp. $110-150.

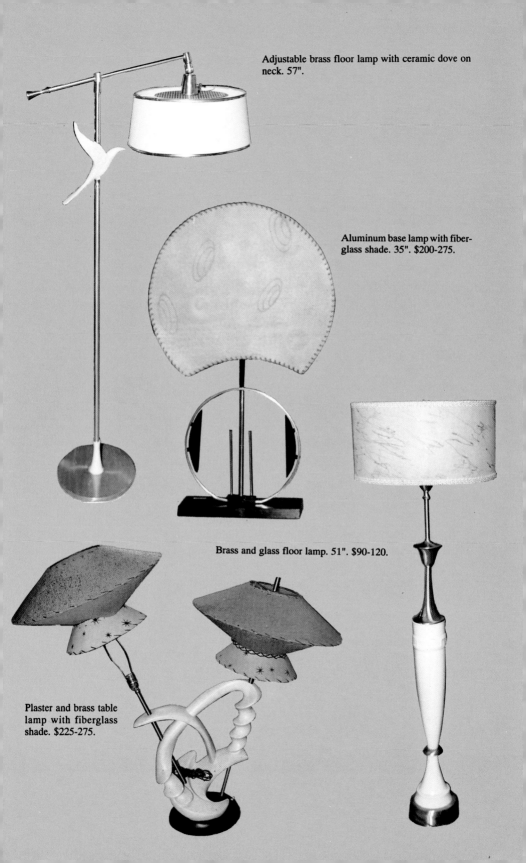

Adjustable brass floor lamp with ceramic dove on neck. 57".

Aluminum base lamp with fiberglass shade. 35". $200-275.

Brass and glass floor lamp. 51". $90-120.

Plaster and brass table lamp with fiberglass shade. $225-275.

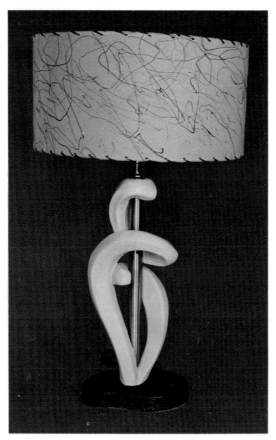

Seashell and coral art lamp with plaster base. 7". $30-40.

Plaster and brass table lamp with parchment shade. 28". $65-90.

Lamp made out of seashells with plaster base. 7". $30-40.

Plaster poodle lamp with plastic shade. 9". $55-90.

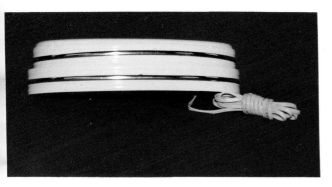

Metal and enamel bed light. $30-40.

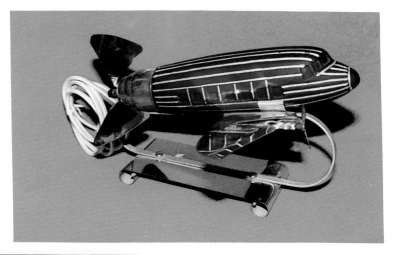

Cobalt and metal airplane lamp. 13" x 17½". $450-550.

Brass desk lamp with swiveling heads. 17". $70-95.

79

Airplane with Sessions clock and Bakelite lamp.
9½" x 21". $300-400.

Depression glass Saturn lamp. 12". $375-475.

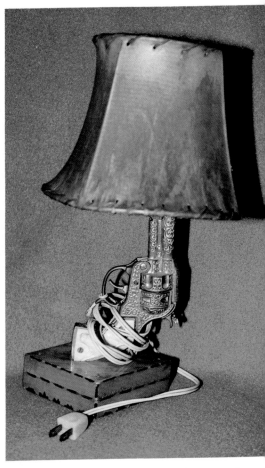

Pistol lamp with leather shade. 15". $240-265 pair.

Phone, lamp, clock, and cigarette lighter combination with venetian blind shade. 15½". $200-225.

Ceramic lamp with square dancers embossed on front. Venetian blind shade. 29". $125-150.

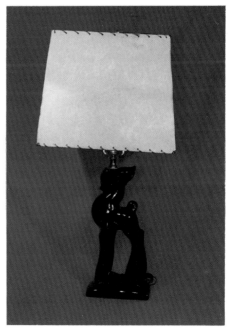

Lamp with black ceramic base and finial, and a parchment shade. 29". $60-90.

Gazelle figure glass lamp with parchment shade. 27". $90-120.

Gilner ceramic planter with brass base. 12½". $25-35.

Ceramic base lamp. 11". $25-35.

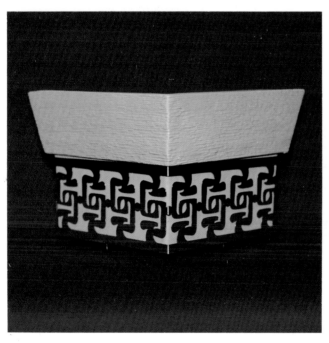

T.V. lamp with ceramic planter by Miramar of California. $45-55.

Ceramic lamp base with brass trim. "Tye of Calif. 1954. "26". $70-90.

Ceramic planter lamp with fiberglass backing. T.V. type. 6" x 9". $35-45.

Ceramic ship T.V. lamp. Plastic inserts to color lights. 9" x 9½". $30-40.

Ceramic deer T.V. lamp. $30-45.

Greyhound ceramic planter and lamp by Royal Haeger. 9" x 12". $65-85.

Planter lamp with bulb behind fiberglass insert in center.
6" x 12". $35-50.

Pair of Lucite table lamps. 10". $50-70.

Venetian blind hanging lamps by Melodylites. 10". $45-55.

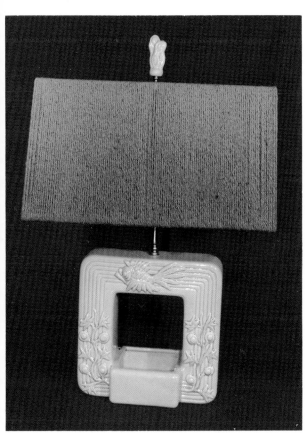

Table lamp with Hawaiian motif. 16".
Ceramic with Burlap overlay. $75-
100.

Ceramic table lamp and finial with rope shade. 25".
$90-120.

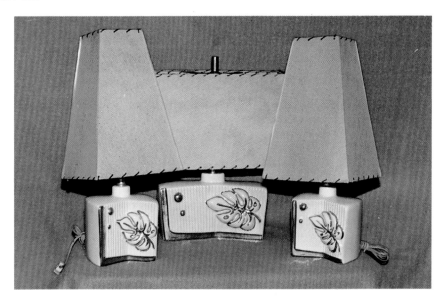

California Ceramic three piece lamp
set. $100-130.

Fiberglass Chinese motif lamp in wrought iron frame. 15". $65-75.

Plastic table lamp with trim bulbs. $150-175.

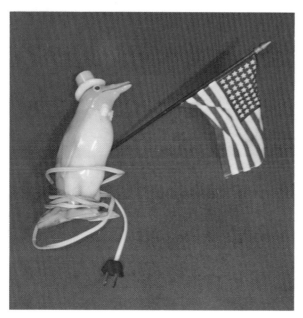

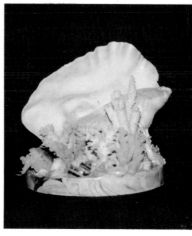

Penguin electric lamp. $40-60.

Seashell and coral lamp with wooden base. 7". $40-50.

Ceramic leaf lamp with fiberglass shade. 12". $65-90.

Ceramic table lamp with fiberglass shade. 25". $80-100.

Ceramic lamp with fiberglass shade. $65-90.

Table lamp brass with iron base and fiberglass shade. 33". $180-240.
Tile inlaid by designer Edgar Britton. $450-550.

Lamp with chrome and mirrored base, silk shade. 19". $250-350.

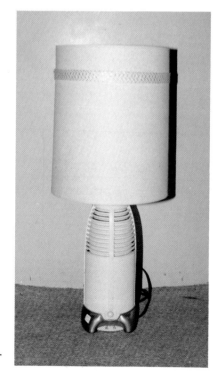

Lamp table. $1500-1800.

Radio lamp, dial in bottom. 29". $225-250.

Plastic horse lamp with fiberglass shade. $295-350.

Horse and saddle lamp with cowboy shade. 16". $145-170.

Ceramic horse head wall lights with burlap shades. $60-75.

Bakelite clock with copper horse. $100-125.

Furniture

Leather couch and chair with wood arms. $1,000-1,200.

Opposite page:
Top: Ranch wood furniture with stirrup pulls and nail heads on leather. $1,100-1,500 set.
Bottom: Three-piece limed oak corner bookcase. $250-300.

5 piece bird's-eye maple bedroom set. Lucite tops on desk and night stand. $4,500-5,500.

Railroad car door insert from dressing room. 6' x 3'. $550-600.

Vinyl sofa by Stendig, 25" x 75". Nickel and glass coffee table by designer Warren Platner. $1,200-1,500.

Plastic occasional chair. $75-100.

White vinyl covered chair with bentwood frame. $125-150.

Upholstered occasional chair on metal frame by designer Eero Saarinen. $2,500-3,000.

Leather cowboy rocker. $350-375.

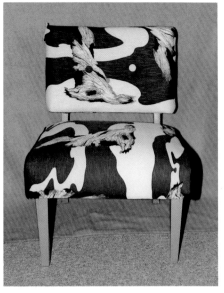

Upholstered side chair with wood legs. $140-190.

Leopard print covered chair, space age form. $90-125.

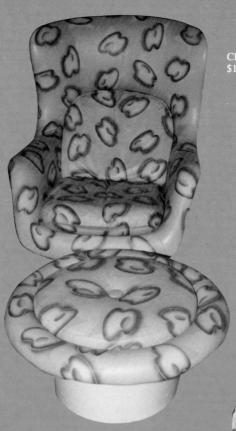

Chair and ottoman, vinyl fabric, plastic base. $1,200-1,500.

Upholstered convertible chair turns into twin bed. $200-250.

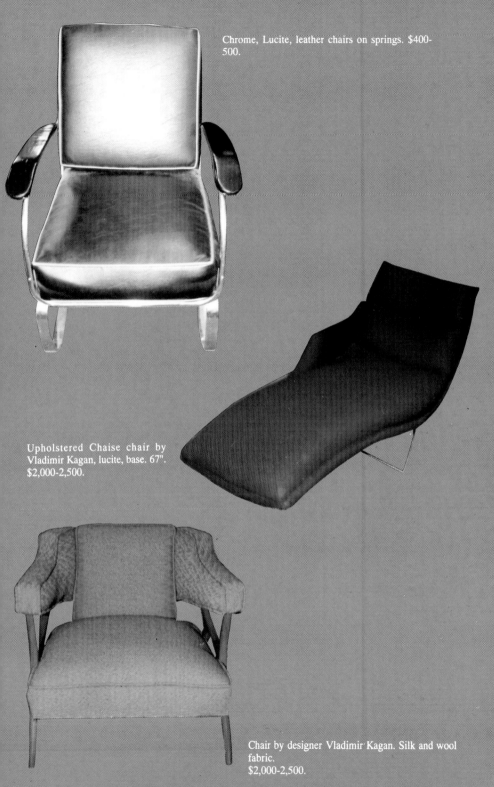

Chrome, Lucite, leather chairs on springs. $400-500.

Upholstered Chaise chair by Vladimir Kagan, lucite, base. 67". $2,000-2,500.

Chair by designer Vladimir Kagan. Silk and wool fabric. $2,000-2,500.

Tiled coffee table with gazelle tiles. $250-300.

Round coffee table with blue mirror glass. $400-500.

Plastic upholstered ottoman. $60-75.

Leather horse head hassock. $160-200.

Vinyl pieced hassock. 13" x 32". $175-200.

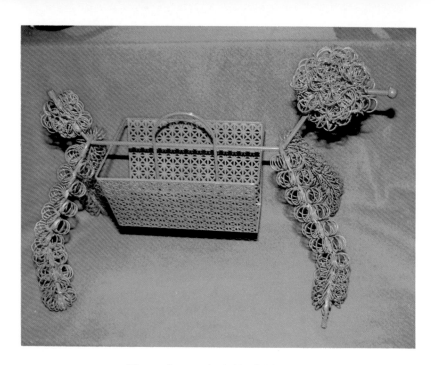

Wire poodle magazine holder. $100-125.

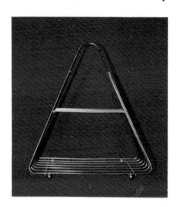

Solid brass magazine stand. 17" x 21". $30-40.

Limed oak magazine rack. 15" x
12". $90-120.

Limed oak magazine rack. 18" x 15". $75-100.

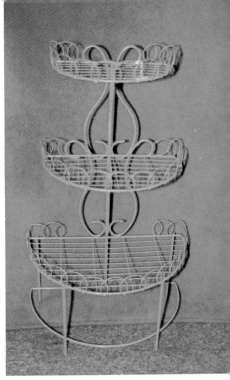

Three tier wrought iron shelf. 35". $60-75.

Wrought iron vanity seat. 18" x 22". $30-45.

White iron shelf unit. 29" x 29". $40-50.

Wrought iron removable tray table. 22". $45-60.

Whatnot shelf of limed oak. 11" x 6" x 13". $30-40.

Formica and wood four tier stand. 38". $75-100.

Display stand with Formica top brass trim. 31" x 30". $125-140.

Soft Goods

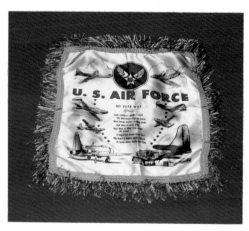

Pillow cover from U.S. Air force. $30-40.

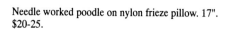

Needle worked poodle on nylon frieze pillow. 17".
$20-25.

Pillow cover, Mother and Dad. Atlas Manufacturing Co. $25-35.

Pillow cover from Fort Knox, Kentucky. $25-35.

Pillow cover from Fort Carson, Colorado. $20-30.

Pillow cover from Hawaii. $40-50.

Pillow cover from Hawaii. $40-50.

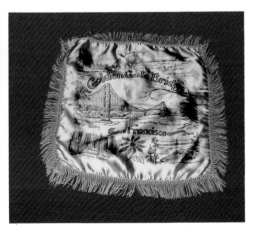

Pillow cover of the Golden Gate Bridge. $25-35.

Woven cotton western motif single bedspread. $125-150.

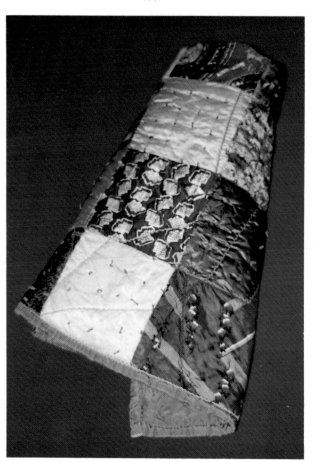

Silk tie quilt. $140-180.

Cotton chenille double bedspread. $160-190.

Cotton chenille single bedspread. $120-140.

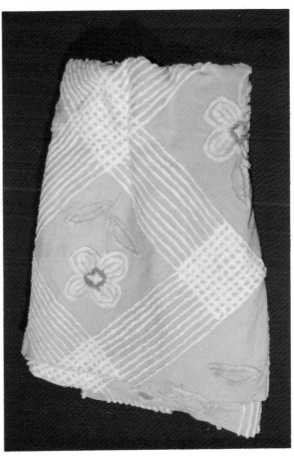

Cotton chenille double bedspread. $125-140.

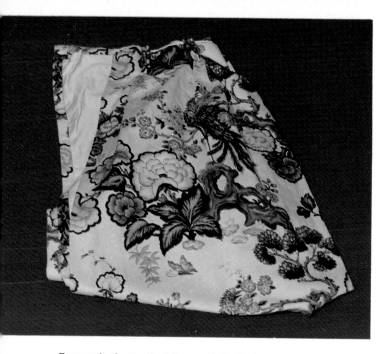

Four panels of cotton lined drapes with floral print.
$40-50.

Panel of cotton drape with scene of mountains. $40-50.

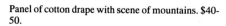

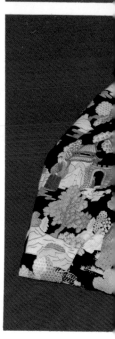

Yardage, cotton drapery or upholstery material. $45-55.

Jungle leaf, cotton cretonne-bark cloth drape. $40-50.

Panel of cotton drape with far east pattern. $45-55.

Floral cotton cretonne-bark cloth drape. $40-50.

Yardage of cotton drapery material. $30-40.

Yardage, cotton drapery or upholstery material. $30-40.

Fall scenery cotton drape. Single panel. $35-45.

Yardage of Picasso-Toros & Toreros, cotton material. Rare. $100-125.

110

Panel of cotton drape with western print. $70-80.

Yardage, cotton draper or upholstery material. $35-45.

Tapestry of John F. Kennedy. 10" x 40". $60-75.

Clocks, Radios, T.V.s and Phonographs

Seth Thomas Lucite clock. $60-70.

Master Crafter, gold tone plastic clock. Revolving lighted fireplace scene. 5½" x 8½". $75-100.

Numechrom, plastic T.V.-style clock. 5 x 5½". $45-55.

Master Crafter, glass disk clock. Brass base. $80-100.

Plastic Librarian clock with brass feet. 8 x 10. $60-85.

Plastic General Electric radio. $55-70.

Electric Sessions clock. The angel fish swim around clock movement. 8". $185-210.

Plastic radio, Zenith. $75-100.

Portable Philco radio. $30-40.

Imitation leather Motorola portable radio. $60-70.

Plastic radio, Firestone. $70-85.

"United" wrought iron and brass T.V. clock with lights on both sides. 7" x 13". $65-75.

Advertising plastic radio from Gulf. $50-65.

Zenith T.V. with remote. Mahogany. 1957. $300-350.

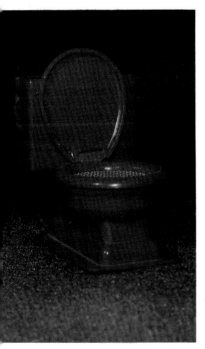

Radio in the shape of a toilet with the speaker under the lid. Plastic. 4". $30-40.

Plastic case tilt Philco T.V. 1950s. $400-450.

Radio and phonograph combo, blond, English.
$200-250.

Emerson phonograph of brown Bakelite. $100-150.

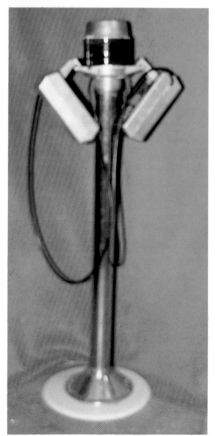

Drive-in car speaker by Reed Speaker Mfg. Co.,
Golden, Colorado.
$250-275.

Record album holder by Platter Pak. 13½". $40-50.

Jackie Gleason record, "Lonesome Echo." $40-45.

Rock-ola juke box, 1950s. $4,000-5,000.

Desk and Office Accessories

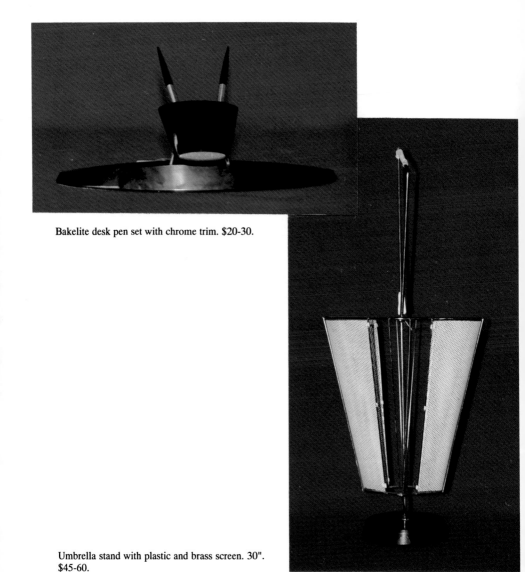

Bakelite desk pen set with chrome trim. $20-30.

Umbrella stand with plastic and brass screen. 30".
$45-60.

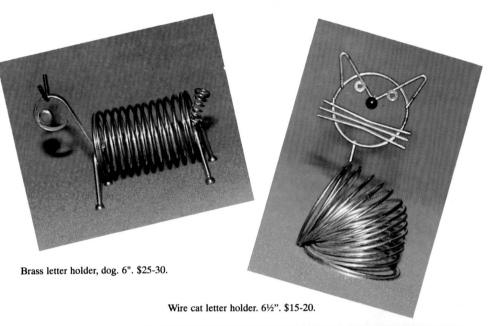

Brass letter holder, dog. 6". $25-30.

Wire cat letter holder. 6½". $15-20.

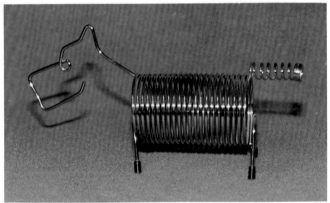

Wire letter holder, dog. 6". $25-30.

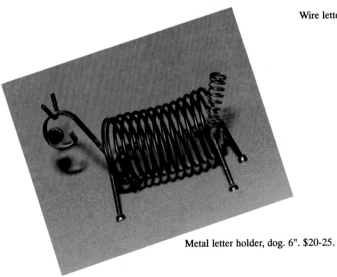

Metal letter holder, dog. 6". $20-25.

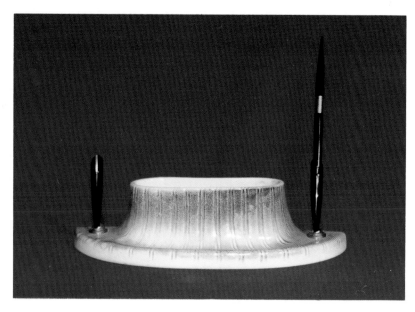

"Parker Spherix" ceramic desk set. $35-45.

Holiday Inn paper weight, copper coated. 3" x 5".
$25-35.

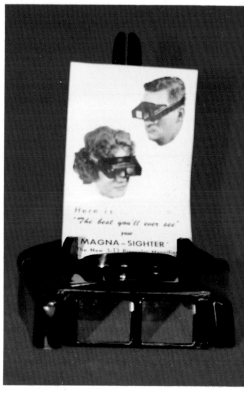

Magna Sighter, 3-D binocular magnifier. $25-35.

Giraffe picture, mixed media. 37" x 14". $70-90.

English chrome fireplace set with four tools. $75-95.

1950s display case that opens from the back 20 x 17½". $250-275.

Toys and Games

"Mattel Baby Small Talk" doll, Japan. 1968. $30-40.

Plastic piggy bank by General Art Craft Inc. $12-18.

Plastic baby rattle by Knickerbocker. $10-15.

Clear plastic piggy bank made in Japan. $10-15.

Plastic elephant bank by Rexall Drug Co. $12-16.

Plastic baby rattle by Knickerbocker. $10-15.

Robot with moving picture screen in its belly. "Japan". 9½". $400-400.

Plaster hula girl, dances powered by the spring in her belly. 7". $20-25.

Shaggy Dog hand puppet. Rubber head cloth body. "Gund Mf'g. Co. $20-30.

Howdy Dowdy hand puppet. Rubber head cloth body. $60-75.

Wire and yarn poodle dog with felt hat and gold chain. 9". $25-35.

Saran Wrap poodle. 10". $25-30.

Hand held "Occupied Japan", pocket games. BB's go into eyes and nose. $40-45.

Child's toy vacuum cleaner by Scientific Products. "Tidy Miss". 32"
$75-100.

Metal fire truck, completely refurbished. $225-275.

A.M.F. Road Master bike with luggage rack. $400-450.

Schwinn, one speed, Hornet bike with Delta Rocket Ray headlight. $350-400.

Metal barn lunch box, no thermos. $40-50.

Astronauts metal lunch box, no thermos. $200-225.

Aladdin thermos with Tom Corbett, Space Cadet. 1952. $65-90.

Viewmaster film inset for Apollo moon landing. $20-25.

Elvis Presley plastic wallet by E.P. Productions. $160-190.

Model kit of the U.S. moon ship by Lindberg Products. $120-135.

Elvis Presley metal button, "Don't be cruel". $40-45.

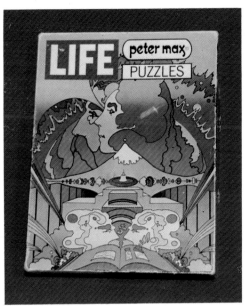

"Life" jig saw puzzle. Peter Max. "Schisgal Enterprises". $40-50.

Art Linkletter "People Are Funny Game" by Whitman. 1954. $45-55.

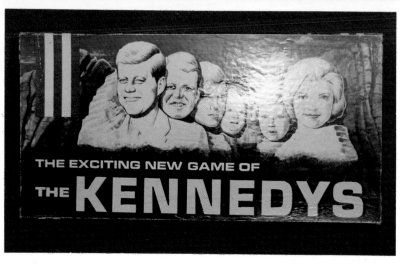

Opposite page:
Top: The Beatles, "Flip Your Wig Game" by Milton Bradley. $150-160.
Center: "Bat Masterson Game" by Lowell.$45-55.
Bottom: "The Kennedys Game" by Harrison and Winter Inc. $45-55.

"Cootie Game" by Schaper. Plastic pieces. $35-40.

"Monopoly" game by Parker Brothers. $45-55.

"Bonanza Game" by Parker Brothers. $50-75.

Parker Brothers baseball game. 1950. $50-60.

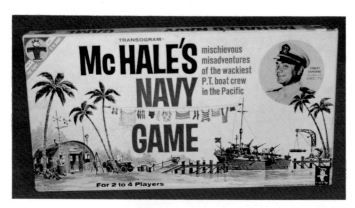

"McHale's Navy Game" by Transgram. $40-45.

Art Linkletter's "House Party Game" by Whitman. $45-55.

Captain Bluebeard halloween costume, Reflecta-lite by Collegeville Costumes. $40-50.

Wonderland Halloween playsuit by Bland Charnas. $40-50.

Rabbit Halloween costume by Collegeville Costumes. $30-35.

Queen of Hearts costume by Collegeville Costumes. $30-40.

Black cat costume by Collegeville Costumes. $40-45.

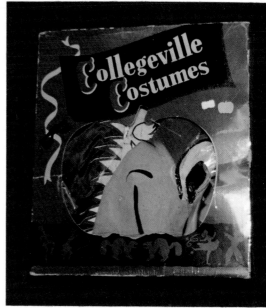

Woody Woodpecker halloween costume by Collegeville Costumes. $45-55.

Vac-U-Form by Mattel, plastic molder. $65-90.

Penny bubble gum machine. The coin makes its way down a maze.
$290-350.

Plastic Davy Crockett pencil case. $45-60.

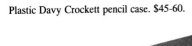

"Handy Andy" chemistry set by Skil Craft Corp.
$65-100.

Game cube plastic dispenser. $12-18.

Plastic poker chips with Lucite holder. 4½" x 8½". $35-45.

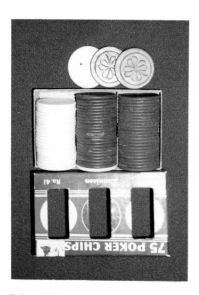

Poker chips by the Dennison Co. $15-20.

Plastic card shuffler. Metal insert. $18-22.

Movie Posters

Tarzan movie poster by National Screen Service
Corp. 1962. $150-175.

Movie poster, 1958, "The Last Hurrah,", by Columbia. 21" x 41".
$35-45.

Movie poster, 1961, "The Grass Is Greener", by
Universal Pictures. 27" x 41". $40-50.

Movie poster, 1959, "The Hangman", by Paramount. 27" x 41". $35-45.

Movie poster, 1961, "The Great Imposter", by Universal. 14" x 36". $50-60.

Books and Magazines

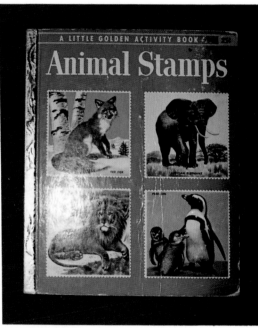

Animal stamps book by Golden Books, Simon and
Schuster. $8-12.

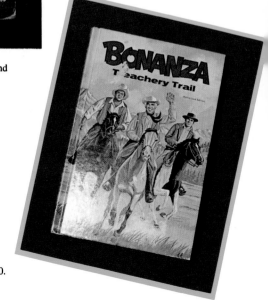

Bonanza by Whitman Press. 1968. $15-20.

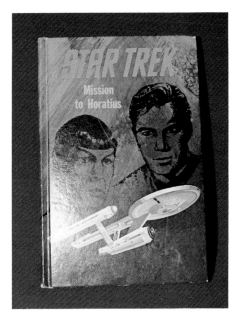

Star Trek by Whitman Press. 1968, authorized edition. $50-60.

The Mod Squad by Whitman Press. $15-20.

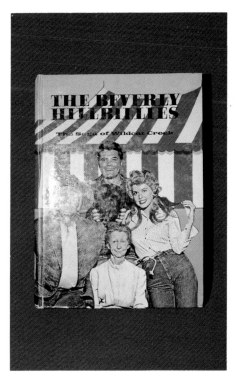

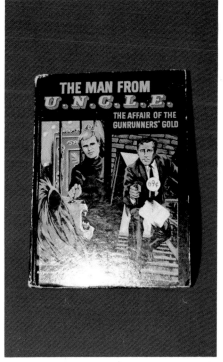

The Beverly Hillbillies. Whitman Press. 1963. $20-25.

The Man from U.N.C.L.E., Whitman Press. 1967. $15-20.

Mickey Mouse and Pluto Pup by Walt Disney, 1953. $25-30.

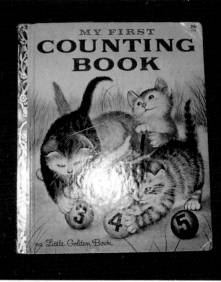

My First Counting Book by Golden books. $5-7.

Seven Little Postmen by Margaret Wise Brown, 1952. $15-18.

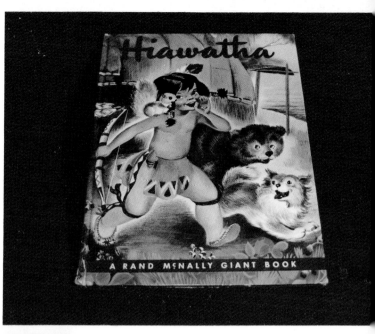

Hiawatha by Marion E. Gridley, 1950. $15-20.

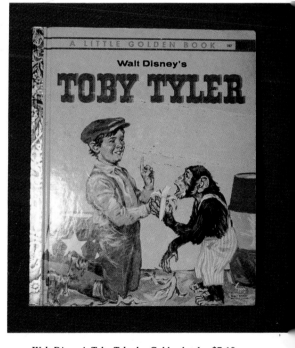

Walt Disney's Lucky Puppy, by Golden books. $6-10.

Walt Disney's Toby Tyler by Golden books. $7-10.

Lone Ranger Coloring Book. 1959. $20-25.

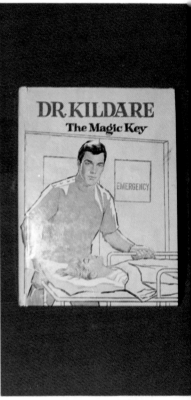

Dr. Kildare book by Whitman Press. 1964. $15-20.

Mike Mulligan and His Steam Shovel by Virginia Burton. $15-20.

MacArthur's Address to Congress by Rand McNally & Co. 1951. $20-25.

Big Valley by Charles Heckelmann, 1956. $12-15.

Series of Cherry Ames books by Julie Fatham, 1950. $12-18.

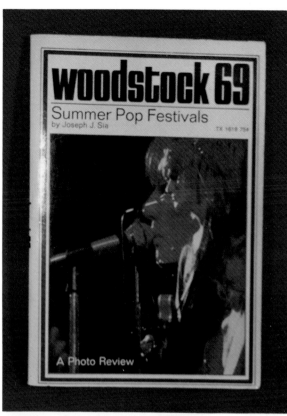

A Photo Review of Woodstock 69 by Joseph J. Sia, 1969. $45-55.

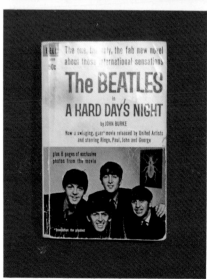

The Beatles: A Hard Day's Night by John Burke, 1964. $150-175.

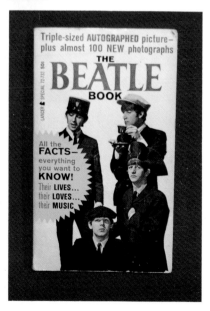

The Beatles book by Lancer Books, 1964. $100-125.

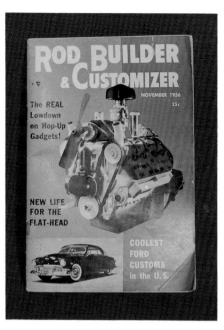

Rod Builder and Customizer magazine by Henry Scharf, 1956. $7-10.

Hop Up magazine by Oliver Billingley, 1951. $12-15.

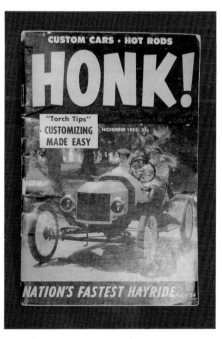

Honk magazine by Robert E. Peterson, 1953. $6-10.

Car Craft magazine by Robert E. Peterson, 1954. $6-10.

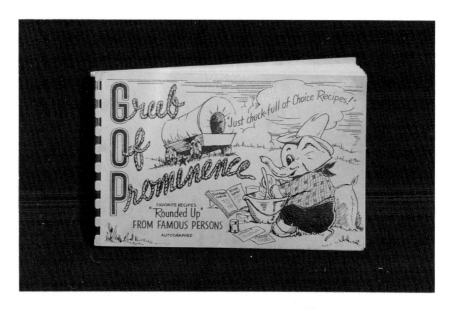

Cookbook, *Grub of Prominence*, by Frank Prichard Jr. 1953. $25-30.

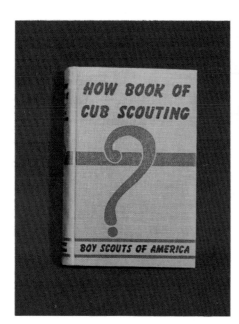

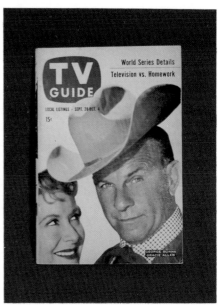

T.V. Guide magazine by Walter H. Annenberg, 1957. George Burns is on the cover. $40-50.

How To Book of Cub Scouting by Boy Scouts of America, 1957. $18-22.

Playboy magazine, June, 1968. $30-40.

Playboy magazine, December, 1969. $25-35.

Playboy magazine, August, 1955. $45-55.

Sports Illustrated magazine. Feb., 1957. $12-18.

Sports Illustrated magazine. Sept., 1957. $12-15.

Miscellaneous

Spring book holder with wood and stainless steel.
$25-30.

Queen Elizabeth Coronation, match book cover.
$18-20.

Salesman's felt sample, "Champ Hats". Cardboard box. $45-55.

Pan-Am 747 match book, with origami air plane. 1969. Rare. $55-65.

Salesman's felt sample, "Dobbs 5th Ave. N.Y. hats". Metal box. $75-85.

Salesman's felt sample. "Knox Hats". Cardboard box. $50-60.

Salesman's plastic sample, "Stetson Hats". Metal box. $65-75.

Salesman's plastic sample. "Stetson". Metal box. $65-75.

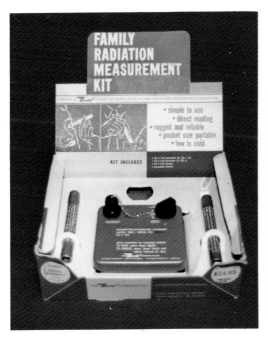

Family radiation kit. Dosimeter/Ratemeter Charger. $60-85.

Coronation of Queen Elizabeth, pin tray, Paragon. $45-55.

Boy Scout calendar, 1958. $65-85.

Coronation of Queen Elizabeth, glass trivet. $40-50.

Stainless steel and Lucite swan hood ornament. $25-35.

Queen Elizabeth coronation tray. "1953 Co. S.W.". 12" x 16". $45-55

"Globel" bottle stoppers in ceramic holder. $75-85.

1958 World's Fair copper plated dish. 6".
"Bruxelles". $15-20.

Fluted glass, 1964 New York World's Fair dish. $25-
35.

Art show poster from Paris signed by the artist Miro.
31 x 24. $450-500.

"Town Square" by artist Cobelle. 14" x 15". $300-400.

"Street Scene" by artist Cobelle. 14" x 15". $300-400.

Humorous Christmas cards, original box. Three-dimensional. "Hit Parade". $4-5.

Christmas cards in original box. Three-dimensional. $4-5.

"Just for Fun" three-dimensional greeting cards. $4-5.

Humorous greeting cards, original box. Three-dimensional, "Hit Parade". $4-5.

Dr. Pepper 1963 cardboard advertising poster. 15"
x 25". $40-55.

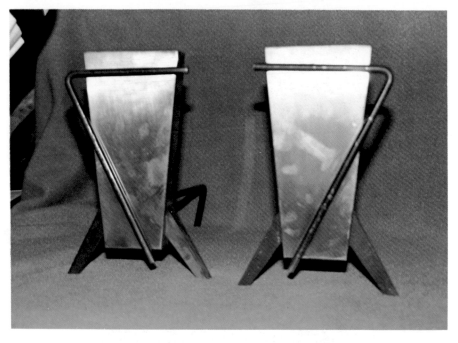

Andirons, brass and wrought iron. 12 x 5". $80-
100.